THE CHILD HEALTH AND SCIENCE
[A RURAL INDIAN OUTLOOK]

Dr Rajatsubhra Mukhopadhyay

MBBS,DCH,MD,Expert in Allergy and Nutrition.

[SRIDOCTOR]

SRI YOGA CENTER [A Vedic Research Centre]

KUNARPUR, SIHAR, BANKURA

PIN 722161, WEST BENGAL INDIA.

Contacts:

https://www.sridoctor.com

E –mails:

dr_rajatsubhra@sridoctor.com

dr_rajatsubhra@yahoo.com

Phone: (+91) 9732948496

REVISED IN 2021.

Product details
FIRST EDITION : 27 MAY 2021

Paperback:

- **Publisher:** CreateSpace Independent Publishing Platform;
  - First Edition:(27 May 2014)
- **[CreateSpace. 4900 LaCross Road.North Charleston. SC 29406.USA]**

AN AMAZON COMPANY:

http://www.amazon.com/gp/help/customer/display.html

- **Language:** English
- **ISBN-10:** 1499664486
- **ISBN-13:** 978-1499664485
- **Product Dimensions:** 0.2 x 21.3 x 27.6 cm

ACKNOWLEDGEMENT

First of all I will pay my gratitude to my family members for the continuous support. My little patients' parents are also subjects to the tributes. Thanks you so much to the all team members of CREATE SPACE [now Amazon Kindle], who has provided this platform to a doctor of a furthest corner in the world at a village of India like developing country. Thank you also to the GOOGLE to provide the scope to gather data, interaction and images in different other cases .

I need a bit of support from the world morally, technically and financially to carry on this type of works staying at a poor village.

Dr Rajatsubhra Mukhopadhyay MD.

SRI YOGA CENTER,

KUNARPUR, WEST BENGAL,INDIA.

https://www.sridoctor.com

PREFACE

I have come to this rural area just to feel and try to make solutions of the factors regarding the child health. This book contains the topics which were published in 'Pediatrics' forum of 'Nature' serially. All are related with science, child health and some completely different outlook, which may be philosophical or Indian. Here those are given with photos and with some modification. I hope everybody specially the people of science who like the peace and love will find interest in this book. This book's topics, presentation and effort all are based over ongoing topics. Though there are many spelling, grammatical and syntax mistakes. Hope the reader will excuse these errors for the messages that this book carry. In next edition, these are supposed to be corrected.

Being a doctor entering into a completely different world of art and technique of edition, creation of cover and presentation is really a tough job. There are many nice pictures. Many Photos of Indian scientists are given here. The cost is minimum. This is first time when a doctor has been published about many a scientific issue found around the rural areas in India working at his area by himself.

First of all I will pay my gratitude to my family members for the continuous support. My little patients' parents are also subjects to the tributes. Thanks you so much to the all team members of CREATE SPACE, who has provided this platform to a doctor of the furthest corner in the world at a village of India like developing country. Thank you also to the GOOGLE to provide the scope to gather data, interaction and images in different other cases.

We need a bit of support from the world to carry on this type of works staying at a poor village.

Dr Rajatsubhra Mukhopadhyay MD.

Publication Date: 27 May 2014
FIRST EDITION : 27 MAY 2021

All These Articles Were Published In The Paediatrics Forum In Nature Network.

Afterwards Not Any Impulse Arose In Mind To Put Any Matter In Front Of Scientific World. As At That Period I Was Completing My One Post Graduate Degree. And I Detached From That Great Network. Recently The Idea Came To Publish All These As A Book. And Here Is That Book. I Think This Will Feed All Thoughtful Minds. A Number Of Issues Regarding Science And Rural India Have Been Discussed. And Which Will Ultimately Help The Whole Mankind.
Dr rajatsubhra Mukhopadhyay.MD,DCH.

CONTENTS

AN INDEPENDENT RESEARCHER

Entomology is a popular science today. But in an age when science was not so developed, it was quite difficult to study this subject. Specially for a scientist from a rural setup independently. Still when a person become a 'born scientist', it matters little for him. He does not care how many works of him is getting published or reviewed or how many lectures he is delivering or how many rewards he is being awarded. Still his work is unique & pioneering. Such a famous scientist was Mr Gopal Chandra Bhattacharya. He had some unique contributions in entomology. His simple life style & quest for the scientific researches as an Independent scientist face many a problems like his time schedule, fund & most important is the ethical permission and the publication of his works. As today everything is institutional & most of the works are so expensive that there are a few who have a time to think about this. Still, some fields are there like Mathematics, Theoretical Physics, Clinical approach etc, where independence is possible. I think regarding publication, every publication company has a panel board. They can review these papers or make this open to review in 'review -response section'(if at all this could be created) before publication. And they can justify also whether the work/idea can be ethically permitted. This can help many innovative works & scientists

বিজ্ঞানী ডাঃ গোপালচন্দ্র চট্টোপাধ্যায়

The famous Louis Pasteur contributed innovatively in medical world. He was not a doctor.

TREND OF DISEASES

Kotha Silpi SaratChandra Chottopadhyay a great Bengali writer wrote a beautiful story of Lalu. Lalu was a brave boy. At his village there was an epidemic of 'OlaOtha/ VedBomon/Antrik'[Cholera]. At that period there was no known treatment for Cholera and an old lady died from that. Lalu spent a whole night with her dead body in a rainy night of winter. At the dawn when people came for that lady's funeral, they noticed that the dead body was moving under a rag, it swelled up. They became afraid. Suddenly they saw the body sat over the cot. Then they tried to run away. After repeated call of Lalu they again came back. Lalu was laughing. Every body was afraid. Lalu replied that he spent a whole night with that body, because in Hindu system one should stay with a dead body till funeral.

Today this is story. But once this was a fact. Being a doctor even I have not seen many a disease that we read in the book, like Small pox, Diphtheria, tertiary stage of Syphilis.

This is mainly for immunization. Immunization is a nice achievement of Medical Science. It was started in ancient India first. After a long saga it has come back in Medical Science through the England.

Please read https://www.intechopen.com/books/vaccines-the-history-and-future/introductory-chapter-the-journey-of-vaccines-the-past-and-the-present

ASPER THIS BOOK

"However, the term smallpox is an English term for the disease, introduced first in India during the British rule and before it was known as the Masurika (For about 2000 years as mentioned in Charak and Sushruta Samhita before the Christian era) Basanta roga (Paproga, Sitalika, Sitala, Gunri, and Guli) or the spring disease in

Eastern India. The concept of variolation or inoculation moved from India to the England in the early eighteenth century or 1721 by the British Lady Mary Wortley Montagu, who was living in Ottoman Empire (1716–1718) and communicated to her friend in Britain (Miss Sarah Chiswell, who died of smallpox 9 years later) about this technique by letters [2, 5]. Even in 1731 one British called Robert Coult in Bengal wrote a letter to Dr. Oliver Coult in England describing the procedure of variolation used in India to protect the local population from smallpox [6]. Dr. Edward Ives (1773), a British naval surgeon, also observed the procedure of variolation as described by the Robert Coult on his visit to India (Bengal) in 1755 [6]. Before the introduction of variolation/inoculation in England in the sixteenth century the burden of infectious diseases including smallpox, measles, whooping cough, dysentery, scarlet fever, influenza, and pneumonia accounted for the death of more than 30% children of age below 15 years as the record. The concept of variolation/inoculation was introduced in North America in 1721. By 1777, George Washington, ordered that all the soldiers and recruits of his army should be inoculated/variolated. Thus introduction of the concept of variolation was the first step towards the development of Edward Jenner's cowpox/smallpox vaccine, modern day vaccines, and the introduction of the concept of vaccination to fight against infectious diseases."

However, thanks to our Medical Science, thanks to those scientists who discovered its remedies. Thanks to Dhanwantari, the Indian God of Health Science, thanks to Brahmin cult those nourished this culture with Goddess Mata Sitala, thanks to Dr EDWARD JENNER who discovered the vaccine first in modern day against Small Pox, Thanks to Great LUIS PASTEUR for the concept of Rabies and other vaccines.

MOTHER, BABY & THE NATURE

Mother is everything for a newborn. From the birth their feeding, nourishment up to the safety each & every corner is supported by a mother in a family. Not only in human society, also in animal kingdom this same approach we can see. Today this is more beautifully seen by some TV-Channels, like 'The National Geography', 'The Discovery', 'The Animal Kingdom'. How much interesting is that to see that the same sense, same consciousness, same sentiments are equally present in the mothers of sub human species as well.

In a general sense 'mother' is place for infinite affection & security.

If we put this same properties in inanimate world also we could feel starting from the earth's nature, in solar system, in the universe within the innumerable interactions of different particles, forces & energies we are surviving. Millions on neutrinos, photons, rays & waves are crossing ourselves every moments, still we are surviving. We could tell this as 'survival of the fittest', there might have a 'struggle for existence', still we are safe. As if the whole universe is designed in a manner where we are safe, and we have our foods. This is an 'universal mother ship'. Which is eternal.

For this reason we Indians call our country 'mother India'. We worship the universe as mother god. This is a state of mind where though we are addressing the country, nature and the Universe as 'mother' but there is no relation of human body but her qualities & the nature.

Wish this 'Eternal Universal Mothership' be always present forever, for all the nations in the world, for all the humans, for each & every species in the world.

BORN GIRL CHILD & PAEDIATRIC PRACTICE

When a male baby is taking birth it is welcome to the family member. For the second one, if they at all wish, they do wish for a girl. If it does not happen, no matter.

When the first baby is a girl, they wish very much for a male baby. If not, they try for the third issue, again if she is a girl, the mental condition of the family member[in many families becomes miserable. The condition of a pediatrician is also become very distressing. Because, in some families, the members do not take much care to that baby ....this is the situation of Rural India.

Why is this happening?

1. **Indian Hindu system** says, if no male child is in family, the continuation of species for that family will be abolished. This is a fact not only for the Hindus but for the others as well. Because marriage system in society is such where a girl ultimately loses her surname & she is addressed with her husband's surname. She is now a member of husband's family. So long she her[wife's] parents are alive, their baby will be equally accepted by the both sides but from the next generation, the grand son/daughter will be grown up in his/her father's house & will be more inclined /easier in father's house, not in maternal uncle's house. & from then detachment grows. After the demise of parents also, a lady loses interest to go to her father's house. Thus slowly the continuation is ceased.

2. **According to Government's act**, sex determination is prohibited. But they do not follow the rule. They take another chance.

Ultimately the effect is coming upon the new born. As spacing is not properly maintained[for their hurried desire of another issue], mother's nutrition is not well, the baby is small. As the newborn is female, & she is LBW[low birth weight baby], her care is more warned but not done.

3. **The financial condition** is not always is up to the mark. And more than two babies leads to more financial challenge.

Rather, if scientifically is every family would have either single child male/female as per parent's desire or two children one male one female is done, this society will face fewer problems.

India Government has made this rule to stop the girl child abortion. To keep the male :female child ratio equal. As in some part of the country still girl child abortion is present, a sort of barbarian culture. But this is not applicable in all over the country. Specially, regarding the Bengali sentiment I know, they equally desire for the both male & female child.

The generalization of law to avoid some unwanted thing is a kind of immaturity of scientific mind. The use of science should always be to bring out the desirable thing of human sentiment. And the law should follow that strictly.

In Rural Bengal I'm noticing several families are suffering for this law. Eventually their babies are also suffering.

OUR CHILDREN'S TRAINING & AN ETERNAL APPROACH

Today in modern education system our kids are being grown up. Ultimately they are being economically self sufficient & they are contributing to the Nations & the World in various ways. This is good. But what they are gaining for themselves own? When we close our eyes in profound quietness, our inner selves talk with us. I think there lies our real 'second life'. Is not it our real perception? There plays an innumerable imagination, calculation, idea, innovation, ultimately creation or outcome.

Scientifically when we approach into our inner world in a human body throughout the different structures & systems we find the Rhythm. We find a continuous rhythmic workshop of our cells & cycles. Transmission & transformations of energies into other energies, matters to energies and energies to matters are relentlessly going on with in our bodies. Thus, our body grown up, changes in different ages. But within the complex circuit of nerves & brain we cannot search out where we are & what the 'mind' actually is. We could feel, we are not only the summation of mass but mass & energy. We know everything whatever is being perceived by the brain must be in the form of energy not the mass. Everything is being outpouring from the brain first, that is also in from of energy not in form of mass. Still, we could not feel ourselves as a part of energy. Because we are not trained.

Here lies the importance of Sanatan (eternal) approach. Where we are neither only mass nor only energy but of the both but we are different from Mass and Energy. This is Atmon(Soul). Everything is drenched within this Ocean of Atmon. To perceive that we needs day to day practice from childhood. This needs to understand the property of energy, and the way of their action, propagation, speed, dimension. Which definitely will make capable the human brain to gain some excellence which is not possible to those people who do not practice that. Neither this will cause all the brains to express in the same manner nor that man will be abnormal. The manifestation will be subject specific & unique. Before that he should have control over himself otherwise there is a chance of misuse of that quality. In India, China Japan this approach was a reality one day. Now everything is a history.

India is actually BHARAT/BHARATVORSO.[BHA-LIGHT/RAYS &RAT-LIVES/ENGAGED] a place where the people/some people who lives with light/feels/illuminate light; that means their brains were [still in yogis]capable to feel the light with in themselves & the electro- magnetive waves from different places & could transmit that wave to another places.

Hope future world's education system will bring down this different brains using the science & the natural properties of human brains. This will again re-establish the glory of Sanatan Outlook globally.

LANGUAGE & CHILD'S BRAIN

[Figure : Devi Saraswati Puja by children in India.]

[Saraswati: The Goddess of language,art,sound,rhythm,and songs. Sarswati: Sara>That moves/vibration. Swati> being the source and with effusion. That means,Sound which is vibrating. **Saraswati(Vibrational Consciousness in In Goddess form.)has Her Three forms.1.Bharati[with light/ray],2.Saraswati>with sound, 3.Ira> with in body in nerve impulses.]**

Remember any Goddess in India is the active form /functional form of God.

When a baby is picking up the sounds from the atmosphere the brain is getting input of vocabulary. Thus the brain is forming a complex design of word memory. In true sense the brain has no language. We are giving this input to our baby; some in English, some in French, German, Japanese, Hindi, Bengali etc. **Where there is no audible sound, that is in some form of mother tongue or as trained what will be its result?** In a complete deaf and blind child we can study this. Usually for this type of baby a different type of discussion is taken; like 'touch language.' This also creates Memory in Brain. Memory is something more than the effects of sound vibration. When brain is analyzing anything it needs some sort of memory, even in deaf & dumb persons. The mind is actually a result of a nerve circuit where chemical electricity is generating. There is a continuous interchange of energy among sound, light, vibration& electric in normal persons. **In deaf & dumb & blind child , there will be a gross difference of activities in their brain in comparison to normal brain.** What are those differences, should be a point of interest in research to understand the effects of energies input & output in different forms human brain.

That might unveil many unanswered questions of extra ordinary capacities of brains perceptions & reactions to the external world.

PEER REVIEW & A FEW QUESTIONS

Peer review is obviously important for research work. Is it always good for innovative work or any pioneering work ? There are potentiality to invent something which is unknown and its misuse. But is it right to stop brain's curious nature or innovative nature in the name of "Ethical Permission" and "Peer Review"?
If the intention of the work is good, further research is welcome.
Another issue is 'internal negotiation'. When peer review is done in return of money ,how much & how long the honesty will be continued is a question.
On the other hand the "Predatory journals" are also a problem.
Innovation is always different from the usual path. We should feel its potentiality from our heart . For this type of works I will suggest to write book if they don't have chance to publish in standard journal.
I would expect any suggestion regarding this .

GENETIC CLONING ,PROGERIA & A FEW QUESTION

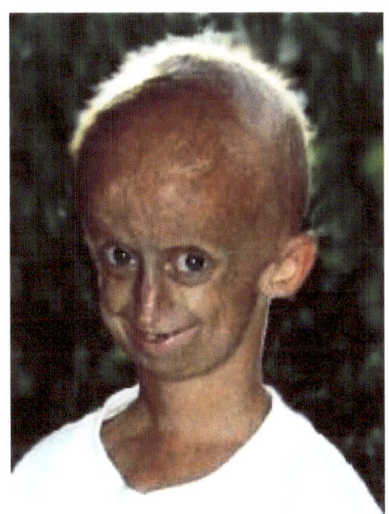

Long time back science has been achieved the genetic cloning. Now there are an ample of instances of cloned life. From somatic cell this is possible.

On the other hand Progeria is a genetic disease where it does mean 'early senility'. Though practically this is not true.

In cloned animals though the somatic age is early, the genetic age will be counted from the age of the cell where from the cloning is done. That means if a cloning is done from the cell of an eighty years old person, the genetic age of new cell will be +80 yrs.

That means the genetic problems of that age will reveal from the early period of new cell.

Is it not a real early senility condition? Though Progeria Is Rare. In Kolkata there is a family with this disease. They are under the care of institute of child health -Kolkata. Specially under Prof -Director Dr Apurba Ghosh.

QUANTUM MEDICINE: A DREAM OR FACT IN NEAR FUTURE?

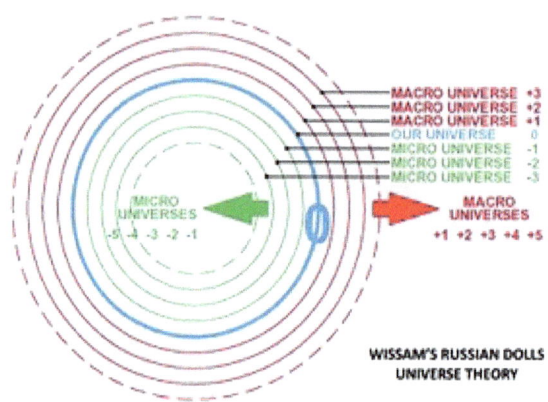

This topic is actually a hunt to find a relation with medical science & nature.

Nature is our environment & something more than that.

From researcher's view unlike other scientific subjects, clinical aspect in Medicine is not always directly related with the laboratory but this needs a rational brain, a keen observation power, and a powerful ability to draw inference. It is clear today, all the manifestations of disease or co-related diseases or symptoms are not fully explainable with today's knowledge base.

The more science is advancing, it is embracing its other branches. Gene, molecule &quantum, everything is coming nearer or will come nearer.

In Paediatrics or Medical-Science also this view point is important.

Rather than thinking this as a separate topic, every disease needs to be revisited from this back ground.

Rather than the existing concept of disease or its aetiology , it might be better to explain from this stand point of Quantum.

In this age, when we have reached also up to the Genetic Bank with genetic technology, I think it will be worth to spend time for medical researchers also with the physics where rhythm, electro-magnetive waves ,laser etc are being used or try to be used to treat & reveal the molecular, atomic and the quantal basis of the disease .

Genes are also some combinations of molecules, bonds, atoms.

Quantum physics' principles, I think , one of the potential application field is gene, & human mind co-relate with this nature, which is also determined by genes. and Paediatrics is the best field to observe this in human, as in this field different genetic variation is found.

I think in future one day will come when like other branches in medicine or treatment "quantum medicine "(I have coined this term since 2009 in Pediatrics Forum of nature for the first time in the World.) will also come to understand & cure the disease.

No doubt the term & thought is of author but the topic is so different that I have no ability to arrive on that field. Rather I'm thinking to ask my friends to think about the topic a little bit. Because it has a potential power to change the patterns of medical treatment & concept of disease.
I shall also ask the scientists of Quantum Physics like Dr Mani Bhowmik -a great scientist of LASER & an owner of a dozen of patents on LASER, to think also about the matter.
Today radio isotopes, gamma-ray etc. are used in ONCOLOGY & also
in GENETIC SCIENCE; but the Photons, Bosons, Fermions, Neutrinos etc's boon is also welcome to the medical field; specially, in
INTERNAL MEDICINE & PAEDIATRICS.
........One day let come when for a nerve disease, no oral medicine /surgery will be given ;rather site, cell & dose specific treatment with pulses of quantum flux is given & which will be with no/ minimum adverse effect, easy & cost effective.
Improving confocal microscopy where cell's three dimensional state is seen , quantum medicine will be given up to its genetic configuration,/ using wave &/frequency similarity quantum dose will be applied even remotely to the specific point.
let us hope for the better days........
.......i will be eagerly waiting for the readers suggestions.

A STREAM OF NEW LIGHT

1. *DIABETES is a well established metabolic disease. There is no permanent cure till date. But control is possible. Mostly the lifestyle indicates a disciplined, control over the greed of foods & food habit, addictions & regular exercise are the mainstay of therapy which can takeover most of the diabetic problems up to the moderately high level of blood sugar & even without any addition of medications.*

But if we look in a different angle, we see, this is a state of body where body is able to create a higher level of sugar. Glucose is the only substrate for brain activities.

Thought process is the most important of brain activity that leads to creation, interaction etc.

In a state of Dhyanam[meditation] yogies passes hours together; even days to months. At this period which will be source of energy for Yogies brain activities?

In women when they are conceiving their physiology is altered. Like wise in space shuttle man has to modify their pattern of food, work etc. Likewise in such a state where the body is completely immobilized for long span of time, the physiology has to be changed. And Diabetes is a state where the body is capable to do so.

Rishi Viswamitra[FRIEND(MITRA) OF THE WORLD(VISWA)] bestowed Sri RamaChandra two powers ,BALA & ATIBALA. By dint of these capacities man can strive many days without food; his brain will not be deprived of source of energy for longer times.

Is not this genetic change?

When Diabetes is uncontrolled this is killer. All yogies practices control over foods. But in Diabetes brain has a continuous supply of energy. That is IGT state[IMPAIRED GLUCOSE TOLERANCE: fasting 110-126 mg & PP 140-200mg}can meet this condition where life is neither very endanger nor brain is hungry for energy in comparison to normal human being.

Most of the Sadhus, yogies suffer from Diabetes. Even in India the genetic propensity to develop Diabetes is very high .And to become a Yogi in India is very natural, common. And it happens.

Another country has such type of genetic likelihood to become Diabetic ,USA.

Diabetes might be the evolution in human species to have a higher plane of brain naturally.

As such we think diabetes is a result of either production failure insulin or utilization failure of glucose in body. But in NIDDM, this might be due to a state of genetic maturity, where the salient massage is,- abstain from the irregular lifestyle & look towards asceticism.

2. Schizophrenia is a signal failure/neurotransmitters level disorder or a more advance state where the brain could recognize the extraordinary things; but as the patient's vision is not clear about self, the madness happen.

3. Atopy, irritable bowel syndrome(IBS), Rheumatoid arthritis-IBS, IBS-Serotonin – a relation among all these sets-are genetically determined.

……… Every Topic Is Different But Needs The Researchers Attention.

ASTHMA IN CHILDREN AT RURAL INDIA

Though it is well known that the incidence of asthma is increasing sharply in metropolitan and cities. In India at rural areas also it is not the less. In India, a survey indicates the prevalence of Asthma is between 10% and 15% in 5-11 year old children.[1], [2]. This might be because of rampant uses of insecticides in agricultural fields in rural areas as I suspect. This Oregano-Phosphorus are so toxic that even a small amount could kill all the fishes in a pond, & these particles are frequently present in the air of rural India today. I think this level should be measured scientifically & there should have taken appropriate steps to cut down its rampant usages. Mr Kalpataru Bandopadhyay,Head of the Department of Cost Account of Vidyasagar University Midnapore wrote in Pediatrics Forum, " I strongly support to investigate the issue seriously. Air borne chemical might cause Asthma. Further, I insist on the possible impact of using insecticides (through agricultural product and through air borne particles)on human body. "

MY RESPONSE was "thank you Dr Bandopadhyay. I have placed this grave problem in front of public through this prestigious NATURE network, so that international research mind turn their eyes to this matter. "

REFFERENCES: 1.http://www.who.int/mediacentre/factsheets/fs206/en/

2. http://www.ncbi.nlm.nih.gov/pmc/articles/PMC2822191/

MANAGEMENT OF VERY LOW BIRTH WEIGHT (VLBW) IN RURAL INDIA

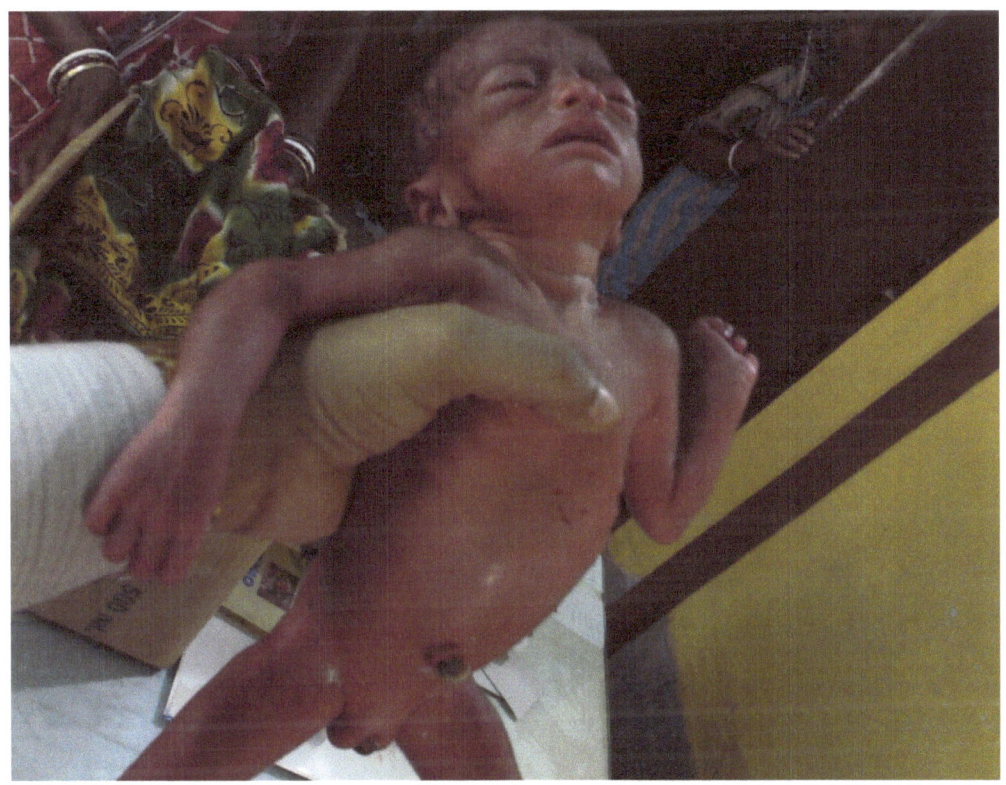

Till date home delivery is common at rural India. According to UNICEF the total incidence of Low Birth Weight (LBW) is 30% in India [1] .This is divided as : LBW, who is < 2.5 kg- 1.5 kg Very Low Birth Weight (VLBW) 1.5 kg – 1 kg and ELBW < 1 kg.

Only 32.8% of this baby get birth in tertiary centre out of which 14% is < 2kg [2] . According international data neonatal mortality rate is 5 in developed country and 53 in least developed country [3,4] . NMR is 61% of infant mortality and half of child mortality is developing country [3] . So to minimize IMR[Infant Mortality Rate]. NMR must to be reduced. Both are linked together. And IMR is one of the three parameter of Human Development Index[HDI] of a country. So to become developed IMR must be reduced. 83 % in rural India are born at home [4,5] . Standard advice is to admit in hospital for the high risk pregnancy and ill newborn [4,6] . But at rural area this is not always possible. And also poor motivation literacy and are the factors for home delivery [7,8,9] . Hence to improve the neonatal survival ,home based management must be developed in India.

Some of them have low birth weight(LBW,-<2.5kg), Some very low birth weight(VLBW-<1.5kg).As per IMNCI protocol this VLBW should be referred to higher centres with level-2/level-3 care Hospitals. But this practical situation is that many of them do not like to come in metropolitan/city to treat them.
As this high specialty hospital are not freely available at rural areas, this remains a challenge to treat this VLBW baby.
If the vitals are normal, with proper advice of asepsis, EBM (expressed breast milk),vitamin E &K, calcium, probiotics, other multivitamins ,micronutrients, except iron they could be managed at home. Even some ELBW could also be managed here. Because temperature maintenance is not very difficult in this climate. respiration should be normal.

But the crucial factor remains is their catch-up growth. Here MCT[MEDIUM CHAIN TRIGLYCERIDES],MCFA (MEDIUM CHAIN FATTYACIDS),PUFA (POLY UNSATUR ATED FATTY ACIDS),&MUFA[MONO UNSATURATED FATTY ACIDS] have their vital roles in brain, neuronal , retinal &vascular development[10],[11]
MUFA has been now a topic of interest.[12] But oral supplementation of olive oils is very encouraging for easy digestibility, absorption low/nil saturated fat content,& easy availability.

REFERENCES:

1.   United Nations Children Fund (UNICEF). The State of the World's Children 2004. New York; Unicef.2003

2.   National Neonatalogy Forum of India. National Neonatal Perinatal Database-Report for year 2000.New Delhi: National Neonatology Forum, India; 2001

3.   WHO. The World Health Report 1996. Geneva: WHO, 1996: 14–15.

4.   WHO. Essential newborn care: report of a technical working group 1994. Geneva: WHO, 1996.

5.   International Institute of Population Studies. National Family Health Survey, India, 1992–93,Bombay: International Institute of Population Studies, 1995: 237–38.

6 . Government of India. National child survival and safe motherhood programme: programme for interventions—safe motherhood and newborn care. New Delhi: MCH Division, Ministry of Health and Family Welfare, Government of India, 1994: 59.

7. Bang AT, Bang RA, Morankar VP, et al. Pneumonia in neonates: can it be managed in the community? Arch DisChild 1993; 68: 550–56.

8. Sutrisna B, Reingold A, Kresno S, et al. Care-seeking for fatal illness in young children in Indramayu, West Java, Indonesia. Lancet 1993; 342: 887–89.

9. Bhandari N, Bahl R, Bhatnagar V, Bahn MK. Treating sick young infants in urban slum setting. Lancet 1996; 347: 1174–75.

.10. Scott C Denne.Regulation of proteolysis and optimal protein accretion in extremely premature newborns.Am J Clin Nutr , February 2007 vol. 85 no. 2 621S-624S

11. E.O. Elvevoll and D.G. James. Potential benefits of fish for maternal, foetal and neonatal nutrition: a review of the literature:Food and Aggriculture Organization of theUnited Nations,Headquarters,Viale delle Terme di Caracalla ,00153 Rome, Italy ,e-mail : FAO-HQ@fao.org

12 . 2012 A.S.P.E.N. Position Paper: Clinical Role for Alternative Intravenous Fat Emulsions.The Academy of Nutrition and Dietetics has adopted this position paper. Their announcement can be found

http://www.eatright.org/About/Content.aspx?id=6442460576

13. Comments:

It was always praiseworthy to think of the own soil. Coming out of the bookish or idealistic treatment Dr. Mukhopadhyay has dealt with the issue of VLBW possibly through in depth practical experience. The case of VLBW is mainly prevalent in all the poor (developing) countries and all those countries does not have adequate infrastructure to deal with such issues as suggested by the standard literature. In this backdrop, I appreciate Dr. Mukhopadhyay very much for offering suggestion to tackle the issue of VLBW.

Regards,

Dr. Kalpataru Bandopadhyay

Vidhyasagar University, Midnapore

West Bengal, India

SIGNALING DELAY OF NEUROTRANSMITTERS &CEREBRAL PALSY

Cerebral Palsy is a static disorder. Cause most of the time is unknown. Some times are confused with some rare disorders like DOPA related abnormality, Arthrogryphosis, some white matter degenerative disorders, rarely X-linked gene related. Neurotransmitters are also determined by the genes, so though direct genetic connection is not clear still genetic relation might be there.

But in CP, there is a wide variation, varied prognosis. Though this is static by degeneration but baby's milestones development are not static, these are slow & incomplete sometimes.

Big question is that whether these milestones could be developed earlier? Then we could combat this disease. Because common people do not bother with the etiology much, they want a better outcome.

Brain is oriented with a varied type of neurotransmitters, signals & waves.

Roughly we could group them as positive(excitatory) & negative(inhibitory).

They have many sub classes. They are very complicated. But this knowledge from research in this field is important to observe the roles of these positive & negative signals over muscle's activity for newborn's growth & development.

In general, I think this CP patient's some excitatory neuro-signals are delayed in extensors group of muscles. If this group is managed from brain's signaling viewpoint, the CP patients could be managed, and other problems associated in a CP will also be managed gradually for this.

Cerebral Cortex:
Localization of Function and Association Pathways

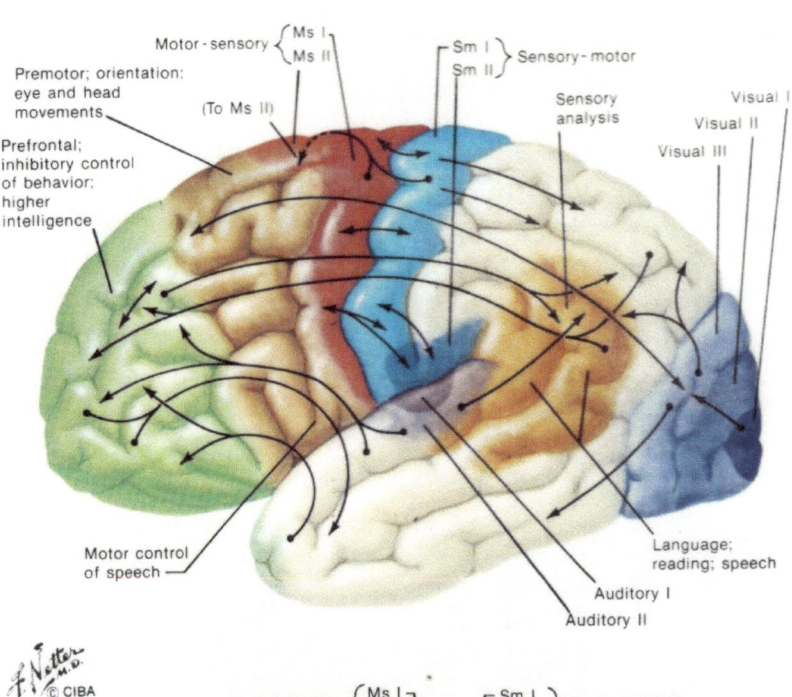

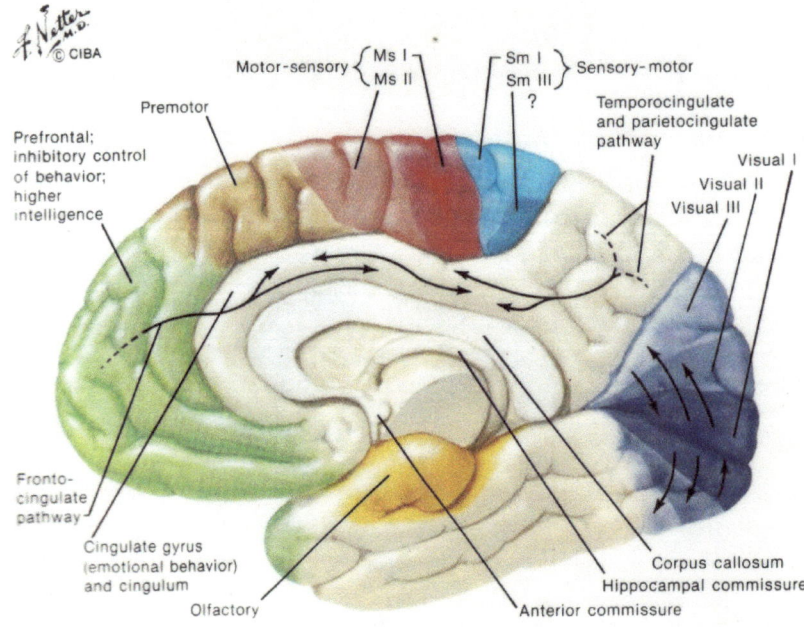

PLATE 10

VACCINES IN RURAL AREAS

There is a sharp difference between metropolitans & rural areas regarding vaccinations in India. In India there are two schedules available; one is of Government of India's & another is of IAP-body's (Indian academy of Pediatrics).IAP's schedule is at par with international schedules of developed countries. This is mostly followed in cities & metropolitans. Peoples here are also aware regarding these. They come to doctor's office spontaneously for all vaccinations.

But in rural India, the Government of India's schedules is followed on , which comprise against 6 diseases; now Hepatitis-B vaccine has been incorporated. All these are being given at free of cost.

But this is being led the difference. The children population in metropolitan are being covered against most of the diseases. At rural areas the public has never been even heard about these.

When any paeditrician is advising for e.g. HIB/VARICELLA/PNEUMONIA etc. vaccine, they are thinking that doctor is making business with these. This is a very embarrassing situation.

Though these are not under Government's schedule, the Government should put messages about these vaccines. As these diseases are also very common in rural areas. Typhoid, Mumps Chicken pox all these are sometime become epidemic. Rota viral diarrhea is also very common .

But counseling only from an updated doctor's corner is a very hard job.

[written in 2010]

MISUSE OF PARENTERAL ANTIBIOTICS IN DIARRHOEA

Rural medical practitioners are the unavoidable facts in rural India now. They are mostly coming up from different doctor's chambers, who were assisting the doctors before hands as an office boy, from their qualification, hardly they have passed school final; but long /short connectivity with the doctors make them mentally free to use of the medicines.

They are popular because they are plenty & available by day and night. And they are cheap.

The medicine is also available in India freely, without registered prescriptions.

All these are the pre-factors of using this costly parental medicines in under-doses, wrong combinations, wrong duration. These ultimately results multidrug resistance cases/strains when the patients are shifted to level 2/level-3 care centers.

Rota viral diarrhea is a self limiting condition & what is required is assurances & correct amount of fluids, feeds some supportive measures. Some times it takes more than 7 days to cease. This is very common in children in India.

But what this quacks do is rampant use of parental antibiotics in under dosages from the beginning. This is a very alarming situation in rural India. Most doctors have their understanding with these quacks. They indulge their works. And it is now almost granted that diarrhea means they have to start parental antibiotics.

I think this quacks should be properly trained & right massage is to given to the public.

REVIEW OF THE MILE STONES

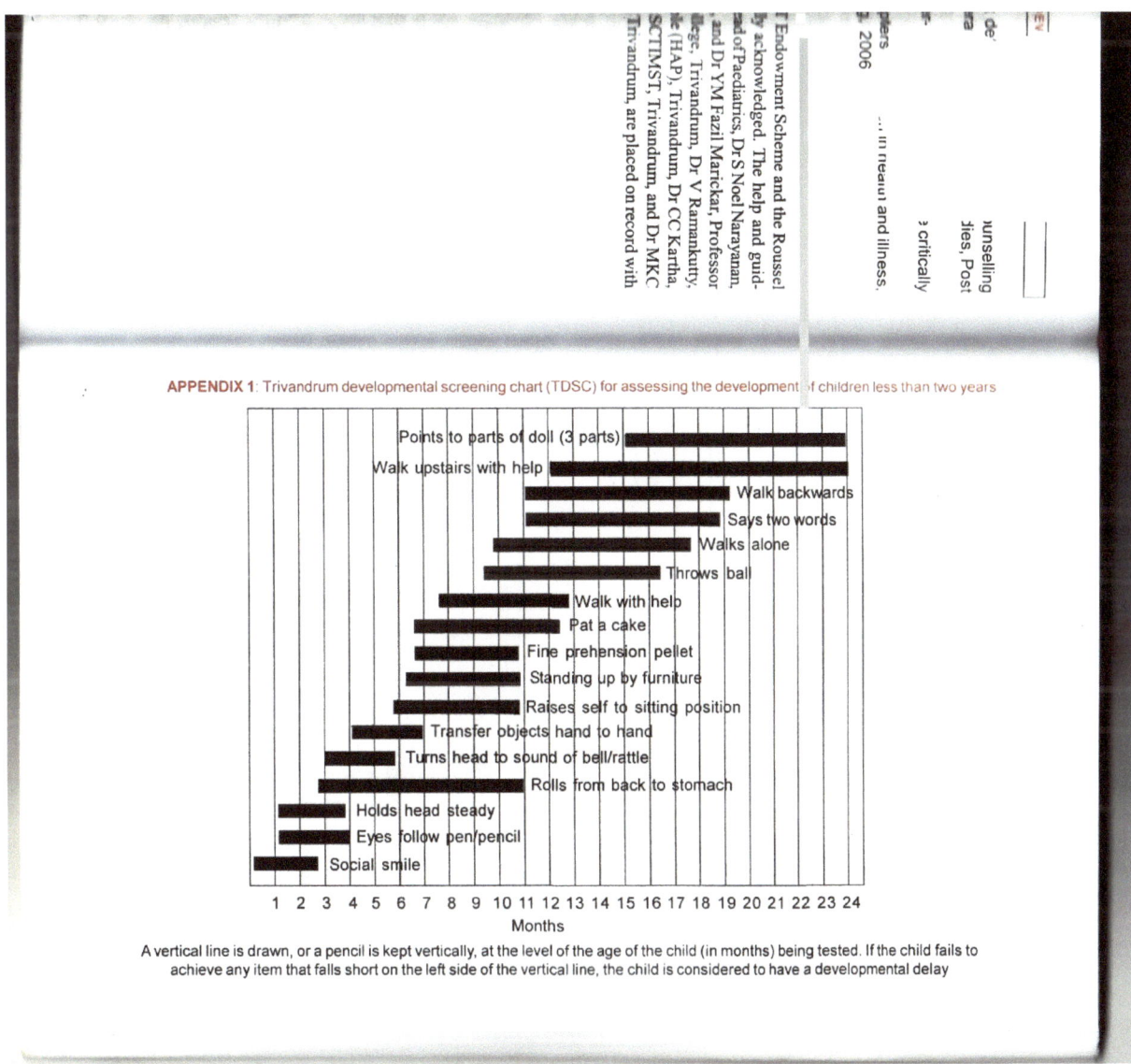

APPENDIX 1: Trivandrum developmental screening chart (TDSC) for assessing the development of children less than two years

A vertical line is drawn, or a pencil is kept vertically, at the level of the age of the child (in months) being tested. If the child fails to achieve any item that falls short on the left side of the vertical line, the child is considered to have a developmental delay

When mile stones were compiled to determine a baby's progress in growth at that period this much explosion in media [mobile, TV, computer]was not there.

More than two hundred normal babies I have observed, their adaptability are much earlier than the age given in the text books. This interesting fact should demand further research to observe whether this is a variation or progress of the human brain due to advanced environment in the family. Planned pregnancy, usage of folic acid, pre & post natal usage of w3,w6 fatty acids to mother & baby all are probably contributing in advanced achievement of mile stones.

THE STRATEGY OF INDIA & A TRAGEDY OF A SCIENTIST

Today(13th October 2010) to me is the most important news is the Nobel prize is being awarded for test tube baby. This is highly appreciable because this is a great boon to the mankind. Thank you Dr Edwards for this beautiful work.

I shall tell another fact that happened in India almost at the same period of this invention. In India, the doctor was Dr Subhas Mukhopadhyay.
**DR SUBHAS MUKHOPADHYAY'S EXPERIMENTAL NEWBORN WAS SECOND IN THE WORLD. JUST THREE MONTHS LATTER.IN SEPT 1978 HIS TEST TUBE BABY TOOK BIRTH.[that means the experimental period was the same.]
THIS WAS A DAUGHTER. NOT SON. HER NAME IS DURGA.**

He was the man who successfully created a test tube baby in Calcutta. And as usual as happens in India, nobody admitted this invention. He was blamed as a fraud who wanted to establish his unlawful child with scientific camouflage. The doctor committed suicide. Afterwards when Dr Edwards established that this is possible, then everybody repented. One film came in Indian market and became popular-'EK DOCTOR KI MOUTH'[THE DEATH OF A DOCTOR].Now Dr Subhas Mukhopadhyay is well known to Indian science. But the destiny is depressing.

Same thing happened in case of Sir Jagadish Chandra Bose during his invention of Radio wireless. Marcony was awarded with Nobel .

History repeats itself.

Same thing happened in case of Sir Jagadish Chandra Bose [en.wikipedia.org/wiki/Jagadish_Chandra_Bose] during his invention of Radio wireless. Marconi was awarded with Nobel .

Same thing happened with Sri Satyendranath Bose [http://en.wikipedia.org/wiki/Satyendra_Nath_Bose].

2. *The particles are indistinguishable.* The number of ways of arranging N, indistinguishable particles in g, distinguishable ways, at any energy level, is given by Problem 4, Sec. 3.2, as $(g_i + N_i - 1)!/(g_i - 1)!N_i!$. Thus the number of ways of arranging the corresponding macrostate is

$$W = W_{BE} = \prod_{i=0}^{\infty} \frac{(g_i + N_i - 1)!}{(g_i - 1)!N_i!}$$

where the subscript BE anticipates the relationship of this thermodynamic probability to Bose-Einstein statistics.

History Repeats Itself.

1.http://en.wikipedia.org/wiki/Subhash_Mukhopadhyay_(physician)

SOME SPECIAL SITUATIONS IN RURAL SETUP and My Modifications

As a doctor & researcher based on rural West Bengal India ,I am facing some special situations, where the standard protocols are needed to be modified.
Some of which are being discussed here.

1.TYPHOID-Diagnosis of Typhoid is still done almost all over at rural India with WIDAL TEST.

Though there are other so many methods like IgM study, culture of stool. blood & bone marrow etc. Still, till date, WIDAL is most widely used.

There are so many fallacies. Anamnestic results may come in so many times . West Bengal is endemic area for Typhoid; specially ,the rural areas.

THERE IS NO STANDARD LOCAL TITRE.

SOME USE 1/80, OTHERS 1/60.One Chinese article says the local titre is 1/50.

We have to remember, to come this positive we need at least 5 to 6 days.

But when the babies are coming with fever say in 3rd/ 4th days with frank features of Typhoid clinically, then, WHAT EVER IS THE TITRE LEVEL,WE HAVE TO CONSIDER AS POSITIVE.

NEEDED MODIFICATION- IN THIS ENDEMIC AREA OF ENTERIC FEVER, WIDAL TEST POSITIVITY AT ANY LEVEL IS DIAGNOSTIC FOR TYPHOID[ENTERIC FEVER],IF CLINICALLY SUSPECTED.

2.COW'S MILK -As a baby food here the people think the cows milk is indispensable. But this is commonest source of starting atopic reaction & intolerance in babies[PERI ANAL EXCORIATION, RECURRENT VOMITING, FLATULENCE, CRY FOR ABDOMINAL CRAMP, DIARRHEA,FRANK BLOOD OR OCCULT BLOOD IN STOOL{IN LACTOSE INTOLERANCE-pH<6.5, POSITIVE REDUCING SUBSTANCE}]. This is very difficult to convince them.

NEEDED MODIFICATION-TO AVOID COW'S MILK where this reactions have been started with clinical features &TO FOLLOW A soy FORMULA/OTHER FOODS IS NEEDED AT LEAST FOR THREE WEEKS, THEN ACCORDING TO RESPONSE TO RESTARTING THIS[SOMETIMES WITH SLOW DESENSITIZATION METHOD].

3. **DIARRHEA & FEEDINGS**- Though breast feeding is very important but in diarrheas if any form of milk & fruit juices are avoided then the control of motion occurs earlier.

NEEDED MODIFICATION-AVOIDANCE OF MILK FROM ANIMALS & HUMAN SOURCE & SUPPLEMENTATION OF MILK OF PLANT SOURCE & OTHER FOODS & FLUIDS ARE NEEDED FOR ABOUT FIVE DAYS ONLY.

4.**FEVER**-Ice bag & fever is inter-connected from hundred of years.

How does the fever come down with water? It is the latent heat exchange not direct exchange of heat that cools the body. From the body the water takes the latent heat to evaporate ,thus the fever comes down.

Therefore to get quicker result we should advice to sponge the body with Luke warm water not the ice cap over the head. As skin surface areas are more on body than head. And latent heat exchange process will be more if more surface areas are there. And will become more rapidly steam if this is Luke warmed than cooler one. COOLING THE HEAD/WATER OVER HEAD MIGHT CAUSE MORE BRONCHO SPASM IN RESPIRATORY INFECTION,WHICH USUALLY IS ASSOCIATED WITH FEVER & OR MIGHT PRECIPITATE RESPIRATORY SYMPTOMS.

Direct cooling can not lower down a central endogenous process that happens with the pyrogens in fever.

On the contrary,

in hot climate, where the temperature is getting high from an EXOGENOUS SOURCE ,e.g. HEAT STROKE, there ice bathe is important to lower the temperature.

NEEDED MODIFICATION-TO USE LUKE WARM WATER FOR SPONGING THE BODY IF FEVER IS HIGH ,NOT WATER OVER HEAD -IS NEEDED TO BE COUNSELLED TO THE PARENTS.

5.**TALC**- Here I have seen a keen interest to use talc by the pediatricians[for medicated talc] & family members since birth. That creates more skin problems. Because, with each hair follicle there is a sweat gland over the skin. This remains mostly closed since birth. And the talc causes more obstruction to the passage of sweat & resulting into skin problems. Soap water can open up the passages.

NEEDED MODIFICATION-NO USE OF TALC & AFTER 2-3 WEEKS, USE SOAP WATER DURING BATHE.[ALSO AVOID OIL DURING SUMMER FORTHE SAME REASON.]

6.**PHIMOSIS**-A PHYSIOLOGICAL SITUATION FOR NEW BORN. Here the usual practice is nothing to do with this. But afterwards if family members become concerned about this, they are advised for message the fore skin & in failure cases ,(&in pin hole meatus cases) they are advised for circumcision.

NOW A DAYS CIRCUMCISION IS NOT ENCOURAGED.

NEEDED MODIFICATION-ALTERNATIVE CONSERVATIVE METHODS ARE IMPORTANT TO BE ACCEPTED.

7.**NEW BORN& FEED**- After the birth, often it takes one or two days to have enough breast milk for the baby. During that period the new born remains hungry & cries repeatedly. For this transitional period there is a great dispute in advices. Gynecologist advices not to provide any thing to the baby ,as the milk will come in a couple of days. If any formula feeding is offered then , this is also discouraged because BREAST FEEDING IS HIGHLY PROMOTED. [& MOSTLY WE DO A COPY ALWAYS] .

But here still a fair number of the pregnant mother is under developed. And their baby also becomes LOW BIRTH WEIGHT.

For them an early feed is important. Specially with calcium, other minerals, vitamin E

& EFAs.

If we consider all the situations at a time,

simple oral supplementation of GLUCOSE DRINK IS A GOOD ALTERNATIVE. Along with other supplementations . like EFAs, vit E etc.

This is very cheap, easily available & easy to feed. As a pediatrician we sometimes advice Dextrose infusion for the new born for first two days, then this cheaper energy drink can replace the need to buy a formula feed for this first two days & this causes no hunger to the baby also. AFTER TWO DAYS STILL IF THERE IS NOT ENOUGH MILK [DIAPER COUNTING/DAY & WEIGHT GAINING{remember for first 7-14 days weight might decrease & so this parameter is fallacious for first two days.}], THEN FORMULA FEEDING IS IMPORTANT.

[might be this is a fact that we are in favour of BREAST FEEDING & I'm not supporting any company, still if situation arises, we should prescribe formula feeding]

NEEDED MODIFICATION -TO PROVIDE ORAL GLUCOSE DRINK FOR FIRST TWO DAYS TO THE NEW BORN WHERE THERE IS NOT ENOUGH MILK.

8.ORAL STEROID & PAEDIATRICS-I have watched a generalized panic regarding steroid at this areas. This has been extended in such an extent that some times daily practice is becoming difficult. The common people should be convinced that not always this steroid is bad rather life saving. Today the evolution of steroid has been reached up to the DEFLAZACORT. Day by day side effects are coming down with newer generation. SHORT COURSE STEROID[<7 DAYS] IS ALMOST SAFE & SOME TIMES LIFE SAVING. At rural set up wheezy patients are very common.

This short course newer oral steroid[SCNOS] can lowers the afterwards complications, might lowers several immune mediated complications, hospital admission & use of higher parenteral antibiotics. Therefore a justified use of SCNOS is not at all bad.

NEEDED MODIFICATION- JUDICIAL USE OF SCNOS[short course newer oral steroids]IN EARLY STAGE OF RESPIRATORY INFECTION IS ALMOST SAFE.

AN OATH PRIOR TO A NEW YEAR & A BETTER WORLD

2010 is almost over. Another new year is waiting at the door. If we frown back then we can see, there is an enormous development of science within a last couple of centuries. Today's newborn cannot imagine what was our world even twenty years back. A rapid change almost like an explosion has happened through all over the world with in a short span of time. All credits go to scientists of communications technology; specially in electronic level, optics field, computer world. Even its a fact, I could not imagine even to communicate with rest of the world staying at the furthest corner of the world in just ten years back. Today internet, mobile phone, fax, Skype, developed road & vehicles all have made possible to continue any research work on that area in any part of the world. This was not possible beforehand.

Now I think any elite people can stay for their job anywhere if these facilities are available. ALL THE WORLD HAS BECOME A COZY HOME!
With the help of these gadgets a scholar person in rural areas is not at all poorer in terms of updating of knowledge under any circumstances than a city living or metropolitan living scholar.[EVEN FEW YEARS
BACK A RURAL LIFE WAS A CURSE.BUT TODAY I MYSELF HAVE GLADLY

CHOSEN TO CONTINUE MY RESEARCH WORKS BASED ON THIS AREAS & PEOPLE'S SENTIMENTS. WHICH IS NEVER POSSIBLE FROM THE METROPOLITANS].

BUT WHERE SHOULD WE STOPPED?
Endeavor has no end. Still we have to control ourselves.
Science & technology always have two sides. As in one hand this is a great boon, in other hand this is
increasing THREATS TO THE EXISTANCE OF LIFE FROM DIFFERENT CORNERS. 1.DESTRUCTIONOF OZONE LAYER.2.ATOM & HYDROGEN BOMBS,3.GLOBAL W ORMING.4. DISBALANCE OF ECOSYSTEM BY DEFORTRATION. 5.DISCOVERY OF DIFFERENT LIFE THREATENING DRUGS,LIKEHEROIN, LSD E TC,6.INDIRECT INDULENCE OF UNLIMITED OFFENSSIVE ACTS LIKE CRIME[e.g.
-
DESTRUCTION OF BUSINESS TOWERS IN WASHINGTON,TAJ HOTEL IN BOMBA Y,TERRORISTATTACK IN USA'S EMBASSY IN KOLKATA],VIOLENCE[RAPE,MURDER],PROHIBITED SEX[CH ILDABUSE,PRE ADOLESCENT SEX].7.BOILOGICAL WEAPONS. ALL THESE ARE ONLY A FEW INSTANCES OF TODAY'S UGLY FACE OF SCIENCE.

WHO IS RESPONSIBLE FOR THIS?
No way we can blame the science. Man has developed this ,so the responsibility is to be shouldered by us.
Actually there are two types of mind & people always; good & bad.

The labor room of this divine & devil brains is the Laboratory In Different Parts Of The World.
This Is Utmost Important To Identify These Fellows Around Us. This Type Of important Media Like

'Nature' Where Various Scientists Can Have The Opportunity To discuss Each Other ,Has A Great Role About This Matter.

Different International conference Organizers Should Look About This Fact.
In Lieu Of Rattle Race Of Discovery We Should Think Twice What Is The Intention Of That Work & What Are The Pros & Cons Of That Discovery.
Rather We Should Engage Ourselves To Discover So That We Can Make Our Earth more Beautiful.[e.g. vice to discover the source of energy from atom an effort to avail it from sun, air & space].

Let Us Come Together To Join Our Hands On The Eve Of This New Year.

GENETIC EVOLUTION ,HUMAN& HUMAN DEVELOPMENT INDEX(HDI)

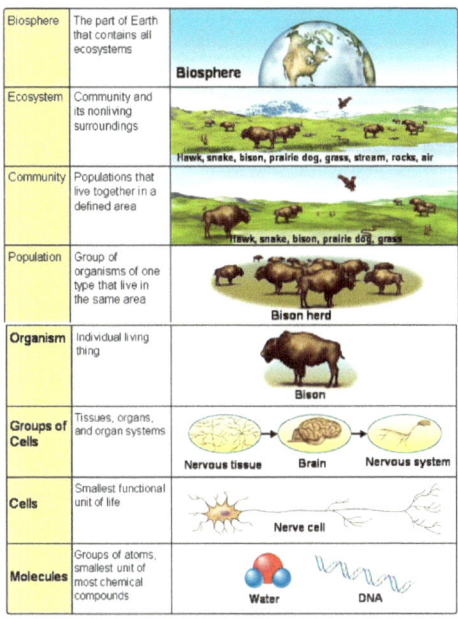

This is our sweet Earth. In the living kingdom we the homo sapiens are the most developed species.

Evolution is a continuous process. From this stage of evolution the changes are expected in human are in two fields,

1. ADAPTIVE[according to the nature's change],2.HIGHER BRAIN ACTIVITIES[creatibility, calculation, imagination, guessing etc].

Human's development is calculated among countries with HUMAN DEVELOPMENT INDEX[HDI].This is again consists of IMR[infant mortality rate-denotes condition of society, health& food],LITERACY RATE[-denotes condition of society, interest for broader outlook],PER CAPITA INCOME-[denotes country's power of money, skills,social condition].

But this yard stick might have utility in a gross materialistic social world. There is a very little connection with human development in inner world/at genetic level.

There are few qualities of human which are same as other animals. But a lots of unique changes are there , which have been genetically changed & for which human is the highest manifestation of animal kingdom.

As in one side there are anger, greed, jealousy, rivalry &lust ; in other side there is Love, Compassion, Self Control, Honesty & Sacrifice. In short we can denote these as POSITIVE & NEGATIVE QUALITIES.

In nature there is variation & human qualities have also variations. Variation compels us to live with different tastes, colours, needs, races & nations.

Variation & demand creates market & competition.

Competition leads to stress, rivalry & wrong doing to survive/to be the best in the market. This market is evaluated in terms of MONEY . Money is therefore the most important factor to demarcate ourselves as rich or poor in materialistic world. Again Rich lives in better life and GOOD qualities manifest more in them and the Poor may do more crime for basic need so there is more BAD people.

On the contrary , there were several civilizations/races/cults who do not believe this type of Market concepts. They are still present through generations together.

I think there is also some GENETIC CHANGES happened. For which though today's world is making them compelled to adopt today's path, there body & mind is refusing that life.

This is stress full to them.

Researches should be done with this human beings. They are possibly the most evaluated types among the homo sapiens.

The more acculturation is going on interchange of ideas, views ,skills, brains & traditions are also going on.

A completely different world is almost ensuing where there will be a clear demarcation between peoples with positive outlook from others around the world.

In every country there is two large groups & like minded peoples will come together naturally.

At this point this HDI is to be revised in the light of humanity & its genetic imprints.

Those to whom we say great men like Rishis, Yogies,Fakirs,saints /Lord Buddha, Jesus Christ,Sri Chaitanya,Sri Ramakrishna, Sister Nivedita[Miss Margaret Noble],Mahatma Gandhi, Sri Snai of Sridi, Mother Teressa, Pravajika Prabuddhaprana & so on. All are the examples of human beings who never gave the money as a priority.

We always likes those divine lives because there we find peace, safety & shelter.

THE WHOLE WORLD IS SAFE UNDER THESE PEOPLE.

SOME WAR MONGERS WHO ARE GREEDY, DISHONEST, LUSTY ,WHO DOES NOT TRUST THEMSELVES, HOW THEY COULD SAVE THE WORLD? HOW THEY COULD LEAD THE WORLD?

Naturally this divine life is the target of earthly life, not the competition in global market .

HUMAN DEVELOPMENT SHOULD BE ESTIMATED IN TERMS OF DEVELOPMENTS OF HUMANITIES & DIVINE QUALITIES ,NOT IN TERMS OF MONEY.

In psychiatry there are two types of EGODEFENCE MECHANISMS,

1.IMMATURE[routes of different psychiatric disease],2.MATURE[by which we behave as normal.] Examples are HUMOR,SUBLIMISION,ANTICIPATION etc. But last two mechanisms ALTRUISM [sacrifice for offspring, nation, country] & ASCETISM[sacrifice of self demands] are very important in this context.

Greatness lies on SACRIFICE & RESIGNATION not in enjoyments.

Money has a relation with enjoyment. Money is important for life but not everything. Enjoyment is fulfilling of own desires.

According to Martin Luther King love is PHILIA[bodily love],AGEP[love for country, nations etc.],EROS[divine love].The goal of human development is the transmigration of this love from philia to eros.In words of Sri Aurobindo ' WE HAVE COME TO THIS EARTH TO CHANGE AN EARTHLY LIFE INTO THE DIVINE LIFE.' This words has no relation with today's criteria of HDI.

Therefore the races in which this type of attitudes is nourishing through generations together they bother very little about money.

This is a fact from time immemorial in India & allied countries. So though today every peoples, every nation is in a global market & a competition is going on; for last two/three generations there is an immense change in life style, daily needs; still there might have some genetic changes within this sadhu type of homo sapiens.

They feel stress in this life style & feel comfortable in their traditional path.

THIS IS ALSO TRUE FOR MANY PEOPLES OF ALL OVER THE WORLD IN DIFFERENT NATIONS[for spontaneous change & ACULTURATION.]

In India there are Vaishnabs, Brhamins, Buddhists ,Jains & Bauls who are habituated with Dhyan(meditation),Jop(unsound uttering of a meaningful letter/letters/words, Homa, Pranayama, Kirtan (singing of a word). You can call it a kind of ADDICTION as they cannot live without this actions.

This addiction gives them positive force to be honest, simple, kind hearted & love to all. They give very stress over character's virginity.[addiction to heroin, marijuana etc. thrusts people to the disease & death.]

Their genetic difference is important to analyze as they are the natural instances of this developed species, who are very delicate & is under threat of their existence.

HUMAN DEVELOPMENT INDEX IS TO BE MODIFIED LOOKING AT THEM .

They are 100% safe for the world & for the eco system [WE ARE A PART OF WHOLE ENVIRONMENT including all species and the Earth ,NOT THIS EARTH IS MADE FOR human only,not like as we are. THIS EARTH DEMANDS MORE FROM THIS SPECIES [HOMO SAPIENS].

HDI, THEREFORE, NEEDS PROPER MODIFICATION.

CHILD HEALTH & PONDS

[The ideal pond]

Over ten years of close touch through practice & research in rural Bengal I have noticed some diseases are most prevalent here. They directly & indirectly affects the overall health & society of these areas. Gross stature of poorer people here is not well, not because of food but for chronic ill health. Mostly suffers from different water-borne diseases, like Amoebiasis, hepatitis, giardiasis, worms, Typhoid & GERD. All of these diseases are related with ponds. Though today water supply, sanitation, irrigation systems are now much improved, the habit of using pond water is still present. This is the main source of water borne diseases. Nowadays pond water is much polluted or chemicals for fishery and drained after from cultivation lands mixed with insecticides. Mass awareness & motivation is poor. Children are also suffering for this reason.

Some ponds should be kept here only for human home use. Where no pollutants will be allowed. All people should think about this issue.

Review Of Education System In Perspective To Modern Science.

In my early childhood I read about Galileo and Copernicus. They confronted a strong opposition for their views. One sentenced to death for his opinion : the Earth moves round the Sun.

Afterwards in my latter life when I went into the Vedas I found that Rishis are chanting that the Earth moves round the the Sun.

[Jagat>one who moves. Biswa >A special Horse. The verse line is,

"Samabortoti Surya,SomUsha Somu BiswaMidom Gajat."

Meaning is The Sun , The Earth and everything of this world is rotating] .

They sing :All the world is one. They chant every thing ,every man, every creature is from One.

The Bible is much younger than The Veda.

It is clear, though one single civilization started around the Urals, latter one branch became separated and developed with different newer theories.

On the other hand another branch remained the same and nurtured with the ancient philosophy, arts, cultures and science.

Afterwards when different intermixing and acculturation happened with a lots of wars and invasions the modern branch gave its numbers of newer developed things.

Today the science has been reached in such a level wherefrom everybody can connect each other in the world and a quest is going on for the ancient heritages of the mankind , not only for a country or race.

With this background we have to review our all the education pattern keeping the whole world and this universe in priority.(Not the country or a small sector) to keep the balance of ecosystem and to create a peaceful world.

We know the child's brain is unique. From the second years of age child starts to copy beautifully [without realising the meaning. Realisation comes in latter ages.] From this period if, something is taught the brain will copy this. Moreover, if culture continues this will remain. In addition, when realisation will come the matter will be very easy to them. This is true for all newer things and approach. In our matured brain which is difficult to grasp.

e.g. 'computer operation'- in comparison to younger brain and mature brain at when first the computer were developed.

Till date some of the medieval age's approaches is still present in our education system.

To start a complete pattern of approach for the future generation from the universal stand point we have to reset our all the subjects gradually keeping the central philosophy in everywhere .**That is….. Everything is one and… has been originated from the One. That is….. controlling as ONE in a larger sphere.**

First of all we have to think about today's

Geography subject.

Geography is still today taught to the child on country basis. We teach the Earth, the Solar system, the

lands ,state wise, country wise; its nature, food, production etc. everything.

And gradually we give the priority to our country first, then the world.

In newer system our concentration should be first to the world .

Modern science will play the major role here. With three dimensional models, internet, with the help of different Observatory science [e.g. NASA] we have to show to this young brain where we are, what we are & the time & spatial relation of the Earth-Sun – Moon. Their orbits ,their rotation, different sky, diurnal variation. Seasonal variation & their effects on environment, plants, food, animals , insects, their behaviours, built etc.

Virtual science & models also have a great role here. Afterwards the land & country will come.

[To think about the Geography always in a brain - a shape of a complete Man-Earth – Solar system in space that rotate & seen in a whole year

{a space in respect to a particular time(day/night) & season(staring pattern, climate)},

should come first .]

This type of approach is always followed by all the Yogis & Rishis in India,Asia and Abroad.

In fact ,when we individually stand under the wide sky and we do feel or try to feel the relation with we individual and the Earth, sphere, the Sun, the Moon & the sky, then country does not come. And there is no role of a country in thinking of an oneness with the universe for an individual. And is the greater fact than our own nationality for an individual.

And this is followed most importantly by all the Yogis & Rishis in India ,Asia & Abroad always.

I think this will create a different impacts on child's brain. They will start to think themselves as a part of whole universe first ,then the country will come.

This is very important for the future generation to restore the of peace in the world.

Because from universal standpoint there are many issues where the narrower interest of a caste, colours, race & a group will be much unimportant. Many struggles, murders, wars will be controlled in future generation with this type of child's brain getup which is difficult to adopt to this present generation.

RMP[QUACK] & Rural India

Till date at rural India there is a severe lack of qualified doctors. People demands easy & cheap medical services for first time, because of poor economy. Here is still importance of RMP at these places. They are also common people. They mostly come from different doctors chambers. But they don't know where to stop, what actually to be done. They should be trained properly & some strict limitations to be taught to them to prevent the misuse of allopathic medicine. Though IMA & some other bodies are their against to them, the situation to be properly evaluated.

ADDICTION[MENTAL ACTIVITY,IMPULSE,URGE & NEUROLOGICAL PHENOMENA]

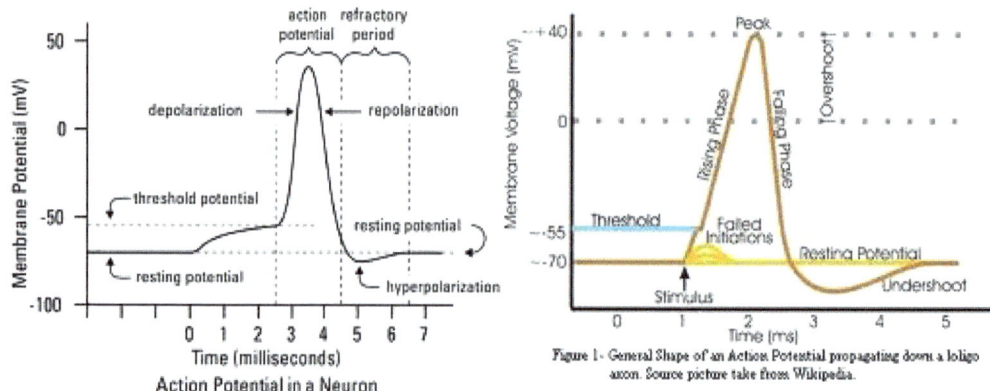

Figure 1- General Shape of an Action Potential propagating down a loligo axon. Source picture take from Wikipedia.

In neurology there is a chapter on Action potential. Every nerve & muscle fiber has action potential of its own. This undergoes through some phases. Recruitment, action, spike, fall, release, relax & normal states.

Mind has the same property. 'Thought Process' happens in the same ways. Result of thac expresses through different types of mental activities. Some of them is normal & and some are abnormal. Some are ordinary, some addictive, some awesome, some frightful, some in diseased state.

'Addictive Impulse' repeats itself. The gain is pleasure. For our MIND we say this is URGE.

Our brain loves rhythms. That means it likes to recognize some specific impulses & try to feel its effects in terms of 'good' or 'bad'. If this feels good / relaxing/EXCITATION which is enjoyable, this makes attraction >habit formation>ADDICTION.

Any situation, any music, scene, story, fluids, chemical, drugs can do this either by directly creating /releasing the euro chemicals /impulses those are resulting this state ALL ARE ADDICTIVE.

ADDICTION generally as we think, this may be in such an extent which is irresistible & a disease state>cutting PQLI[physical quality of life index]> Daily life activities>CRIPPLING>Death.

If we consider its principle of Action Potential, then we can channelize this brain's property in healthier sense.

If we think that property of action potential, if any activity is there which enhance the POLARISATION STATE & NO/LITTLE HYPER POLARISATION then positive energy will grow up.

If we practice that will also be an Addiction. This addiction is wanted. This is healthier for body, mind, family & the world.

This is an age old practice. This is A ROUTINE LIFE STYLE, CONTROLLED LIFE, REGULAR BAYAM[YOGIC & FREE HAND], PRANYAM & DHYAN.

Here again this is the eternal practice in India, which the most of the Indians do not do.

The basic structure of Paediatrics forum was:

This forum welcomes you to all. Come with any type of discussion on paediatric medical science, child related topics whatever you like; if palatable, will be placed. Special recommendation on debates, diagnostic problems & innovations.

This could help the researchers & the doctors.
And also,
this is open for free discussion.

1.http://network.nature.com/groups/nature-paediatrics/forum/topics?page=2

THANK YOU.

I specially thanks to 'Google Image' for many images in this book.

An Effort of a Sridoctor from Rural Set up of India.

This is my humble request

I am continuing various academic works including VEDIC RESEARCH at SRI YOGA CENTER from this rural set up.

If you feel this method will help in practical life and Innovative then please appreciate it and recognize it.

E –mails: dr_rajatsubhra@sridoctor.com

dr_rajatsubhra@yahoo.com

Phone: (+91) 9732948496

FOR DONATION AND HELP:

paytm@9732948496

Please also follow my other works in Amazon.com

.

My Books.

1. INDOLOGY

2. INTRANASAL STEROID AND ASTHMA

3. PICTURES OF DISEASES IN RURAL INDIA .
   FIRST EDITION.

4. PICTURES OF DISEASES IN RURAL INDIA .
   SECOND EDITION.

5. THE CHILD HEALTH AND SCIENCE
   [FROM RURAL INDIA]

6. RAJATSUBHRA'S MANUAL OPENING OF PHIMOSIS.

7. SOBON IN THE VEDA

8. ELICITATION OF COUGH IN YOUNG CHILD AND ITS
   IMPORTANCE.

THANK YOU

Namaste &thank you all,

SRIDOCTOR ...Dr Rajatsubhra Mukhopadhyay.

1.

2.